GAME DAY

Get Ready for a Lacrosse Game

by Emma Carlson Berne

Consultant: Beth Gambro
Reading Specialist, Yorkville, Illinois

Minneapolis, Minnesota

Teaching Tips

Before Reading

- Look at the cover of the book. Discuss the picture and the title.
- Ask readers to brainstorm a list of what they already know about lacrosse games. What can they expect to see in this book?
- Go on a picture walk, looking through the pictures to discuss vocabulary and make predictions about the text.

During Reading

- Read for purpose. Encourage readers to think about preparing for a lacrosse game as they are reading.
- Ask readers to look for the details of the book. What needs to happen before the big game?
- If readers encounter an unknown word, ask them to look at the sounds in the word. Then, ask them to look at the rest of the page. Are there any clues to help them understand?

After Reading

- Encourage readers to pick a buddy and reread the book together.
- Ask readers to name two things from the book that a player does to get ready for a lacrosse game. Find the pages that tell about these things.
- Ask readers to write or draw something they learned about lacrosse.

Credits:
Cover and title page, © aceshot1/Shutterstock; 3, © nycshooter/iStock; 5, © beardean/iStock; 6–7, © vernonwiley/iStock; 8–9, © Tijana87/iStock; 10, © bpalmer/iStock; 11,© WoodysPhotos/iStock; 13, © Johnce/iStock; 15, © bmcent1/iStock; 16–17, © Peter Dean/Shutterstock; 18–19, © aceshot1/Shutterstock; 21, © FatCamera/iStock; 22T, © cmannphoto/iStock; 22M, © APCortizasJr/iStock; 22B, © jaboardm/iStock; 23TL, © ferrantraite/iStock; 23TM, © FatCamera/iStock; 23TR, © Clearphoto/iStock; 23BL,© beardean/iStock; 23BM, © vernonwiley/iStock; and 23BR, © SDI Productions/iStock.

Library of Congress Cataloging-in-Publication Data

Names: Berne, Emma Carlson, 1979- author.
Title: Get ready for a lacrosse game / by Emma Carlson Berne.
Description: Bearcub books. | Minneapolis, MN : Bearport Publishing
  Company, [2024] | Series: Game day | Includes bibliographical references
  and index.
Identifiers: LCCN 2023001370 (print) | LCCN 2023001371 (ebook) | ISBN
  9798888220573 (library binding) | ISBN 9798888222539 (paperback) | ISBN
  9798888223727 (ebook)
Subjects: LCSH: Lacrosse--Juvenile literature.
Classification: LCC GV989.14 .B47 2024 (print) | LCC GV989.14 (ebook) |
  DDC 796.36/2--dc23/eng/20230113
LC record available at https://lccn.loc.gov/2023001370
LC ebook record available at https://lccn.loc.gov/2023001371

Copyright © 2024 Bearport Publishing Company. All rights reserved. No part of this publication may be reproduced in whole or in part, stored in any retrieval system, or transmitted in any form or by any means, electronic, mechanical, photocopying, recording, or otherwise, without written permission from the publisher.

For more information, write to Bearport Publishing, 5357 Penn Avenue South, Minneapolis, MN 55419.

Contents

Let's Play! 4

How to Play 22
Glossary 23
Index 24
Read More 24
Learn More Online 24
About the Author 24

Let's Play!

My sister shoots.

Swish!

The ball sails into the net.

It is time to play lacrosse.

My sister learned to pass and catch with her team.

The **coach** showed them how to shoot a goal.

Tomorrow is game day!

My sister goes to bed early.

Sleep will help her have **energy** in the morning.

She wakes up ready!

My sister puts on her shorts and **jersey**.

She packs her stick and **gear** in her bag.

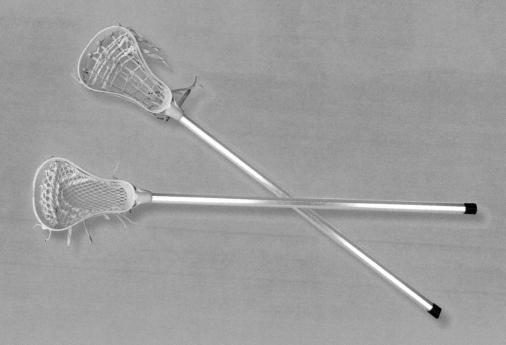

My sister eats oatmeal for breakfast.

It will keep her full for the game.

She fills up her water bottle, too.

At the field, my sister puts on her mask and **mouthguard**.

They keep her face and teeth safe.

The team **stretches** to get loose.

They touch their toes.

Then, they do warm-ups.

They throw the ball and catch it with their sticks.

The game starts.

My sister sits out first.

She cheers for everyone on the field.

Then, it is my sister's turn to play.

She passes the ball to her friend.

Her friend shoots.

I love lacrosse!

How to Play

Lacrosse is fun to play. Rules keep the game fair.

Lacrosse is played with sticks that have little net pockets.

Players get points by shooting the ball into a goal.

One player blocks the goal. They are called the goalie.

Glossary

coach the person who teaches and leads a sports team

energy the power needed to move and do things

gear special clothing and things used or worn during a sport

jersey a shirt worn by a player on a sports team

mouthguard a piece of plastic that protects the teeth

stretches moves the body to pull muscles longer

Index

breakfast 12
cheers 18
coach 6
energy 8
friend 20
stick 10, 16, 22

Read More

Downs, Kieran. *Lacrosse (Let's Play Sports!)*. Minneapolis: Bellwether Media, 2021.

Schuh, Mari C. *Lacrosse (Spot Sports)*. Mankato, MN: Amicus, 2021.

Learn More Online

1. Go to **www.factsurfer.com** or scan the QR code below.
2. Enter **"Lacrosse Game"** into the search box.
3. Click on the cover of this book to see a list of websites.

About the Author

Emma Carlson Berne lives with her family in Cincinnati, Ohio. Horseback riding is her favorite sport.